ABANDONED AND UNUSUAL SOUTHERN ILLINOIS

MICHAEL G. WRIGHT

AMERICA THROUGH TIME®
ADDING COLOR TO AMERICAN HISTORY

America Through Time is an imprint of Fonthill Media LLC
www.through-time.com
office@through time.com

Published by Arcadia Publishing by arrangement with Fonthill Media LLC
For all general information, please contact Arcadia Publishing:
Telephone: 843-853-2070
Fax: 843-853-0044
E-mail: sales@arcadiapublishing.com
For customer service and orders:
Toll-Free 1-888-313-2665

www.arcadiapublishing.com

First published 2020

ISBN 978-1-63499-233-6

Typeset in Trade Gothic 10pt on 15pt
Printed and bound in England

CONTENTS

ACKNOWLEDGMENTS

I WISH TO THANK my loving wife, Bonnie; my kids, Matthew and Katie; and my grandkids, Grace, Braden, Declan, and Addyson for their support. I would also like to thank my two sidekicks, Dr. Terry Brown and Professor Larry Franklin.

INTRODUCTION

This book is about Southern Illinois, also known as "Little Egypt." We do not have the Nile River or ancient pyramids, but we do have the Big Muddy River and a lot of interesting old buildings. It was named Little Egypt back in 1818, and we share the names of Egyptian towns such as Cairo, Dongola, and Karnak. I will show you things that perhaps you have never seen or heard about. Notice there will be no pictures of camels in this book, nor any photos of the "Lost City of Gold," as I have not quite found it yet.

They say older folks always talk about the past, and I suppose that is partially true. I bring the past to the present through my photography. You will see a revival of images most likely tucked away in the cerebral matter of your brain, or things and places you have never seen before. Whatever your circumstances, we will visit abandoned schools, churches, houses, railroads, and other structures covered in dirt, weeds, and debris left behind and hidden for years, maybe decades.

Imagine driving down a road and seeing a shadowy image nearly six feet tall hidden among dirt and weeds. Curiosity dictates that you exit your car, pull back enough weeds to take a peek, and spot a century-old structure. Or perhaps you drive through a seemingly abandoned community and see one block after another of vacant buildings. Again, your curiosity speaks to you. These are the journeys I share with you through the lenses of my Olympus and Sony full frame cameras.

Do you need these expensive cameras to take a good picture? It helps, but it is not necessary. A smartphone such as an iPhone 11 Pro is an effective alternative. I try to photograph my experiences that stimulate your thoughts, creativity, and a longing for days gone by.

You travel down dirt roads, open fields, and enter abandoned places occupied by wildlife, such as snakes, varmints, or a stray coyote—and if it is in the darkness of night, perhaps an imaginary creature or two. You climb fallen fences, step over broken bricks, and walk up creepy stairways.

As with any worthwhile venture, careful planning saves time and keeps you safe. I spend hours on the internet studying the history of communities, railroads, and long-forgotten buildings, and sometimes I find something. As soon as my curiosity is awakened, I go to Google Earth, study the layout, and map out my journey. Despite my planning, I sometimes discover that the building has been torn down. But there are the other times when I think, *Oh great, what a cool find.*

Many of the scenes and locations in my photographs are found by accident. On one such occasion, I was looking for an old railroad bridge only to come upon a river shack standing some 20 to 30 feet in the air on stilts with an old Airstream trailer on top. Sometimes I drive around the countryside with no planning or destination in mind. Snooping can result in some rewarding discoveries. The best tip I can give is to search along railroad tracks; there, you will find many old structures and relics of the past.

I have been locked in basements, trapped inside rooms, and spooked several times by strange sounds. While exploring an old church, I was zeroing in on a good shot when suddenly one of my legs went through the floor. There I was, stuck in the floor of an old church with no one around. While unable to pull my foot through the hole, I removed my shoe, made my escape, and walked away with one shoe, a slightly scratched leg, and a bruised ego.

Walking through an abandoned building with boarded windows is challenging. It was pitch black inside and I was wearing a miner's light around my head. As I walked through the building, my headlamp revealed something blue. I took a closer look and discovered an old elevator shaft. I walked toward it and tripped over something, which left me sprawled out across the floor. My headlamp fell off and dropped down the elevator shaft. Darkness surrounded me as I looked down the shaft and saw the glow of my light some 20 to 30 feet below. If not for the light from my iPhone, the path to safety could have been troubling.

While I sometimes invite friends to share my expeditions, the history of my adventures scares them away. I have tried to get my sidekicks, Dr. Terry Brown (a stout fella with a white beard), and Professor Franklin (a slightly built pipe smoker who walks with a slight limp), to accompany me, but they want no part of it. My dog once made a rare trip with me. My wife refused. But she does keep enough cash on hand to bail me out of jail if I manage to get into trouble.

When access to sites has been challenging, my solution was to buy a drone. I researched and decided on a DJI Mavic Pro Zoom. I fly it over buildings and rivers, allowing me to explore from a different perspective. Being a self-trained aviator, I crashed my first drone four times and nearly lost it in the woods. If you fly it near metal found in an older bridge, the drone loses direction and crashes. On one such occasion, I was photographing some old metal mining equipment and the drone went crazy, dropped from the sky, and landed in the weeds.

Proper equipment is essential. I carry my leather whip, mace, knife, and more than one light, as well as good heavy shoes that can handle broken glass, holes, mountain springs, and whatever unknowns I might encounter. And yes, don't forget the people. Before I go into any vacant building, I always make certain no one is around. Once inside, I am on my own. As a final piece of advice, always go on Sunday mornings when most people are sleeping or going to church.

I have taken pictures of grand old houses, commercial structures, old railroad depots, schools, churches, and whatever caught my fancy. Since I have been taking photographs, many of the structures have vanished.

A common question asked of me is, "Why do you take the chance that you might endanger yourself?" The answer is quite simple. I relish the challenges and the thrill of finding unusual and out-of-the-way things! This is not a passive activity used to occupy my retirement years. It is an adventure loaded with high energy, determination, and engines at full throttle. Nothing can stop me. It is all about the adventure.

While a lot of my friends refer to me as "Indiana Mike," and I take that as a compliment, I prefer "Young Indiana Mike." They enjoy hearing about my escapades: how I climbed the highest mountains (well maybe a tree); went to the ends of the Earth (within state lines); and conquered the toughest challenges (jumping off a rock). It is the thrill of the chase that drives me.

After taking my photographs comes the real fun: post-production. This is where I edit the photo, change the colors, and turn it upside down and inside out. It's amazing what can be done with a digital picture. You do need a powerful computer or iPad with good software to do this. My personal preference is the iPad 11 Pro. The greatest thrill or high in photography is racing home after a long day of shooting and loading the photos on your computer. The excitement builds as you scroll through your pictures, looking for that one award-winning shot.

Over the past five years, I have taken over 100,000 pictures, but have only kept maybe 15,000 to 20,000. I've been asked if you need photography skills to take a good picture. Not necessarily, but you do need decent equipment, and sometimes you have to take risks in order to get specific shots.

A major technique to master is lighting. Remember, try to shoot with the light behind your back, and watch out for shadows! Do not be afraid of "chimping," which is taking a picture then looking at it on your camera display. I think it is a good idea myself. The most important part of photography is finding an interesting subject—something that will cause the interested party to stop and take a serious look.

Anyone can take a picture, but will the person who looks at it remember it? A good picture normally does not magically appear in front of your camera. You must work for it.

Allow the old walls of an abandoned building to talk or share a secret of days gone by. Imagine a broken-down structure as having a soul, dampened from years of neglect and asking to be revived. Through creativity, imagination, and perseverance, photography brings a subject back to life. Join me through my magical journey of photography.

In closing, I must point out that I am going to only give out the locations of public and semi-public locations. All the others shall remain anonymous in order to protect their integrity.

1

BROWN SHOE FACTORY

Located in the town of Murphysboro, Illinois, is the old Brown Shoe Factory. It was built in the early 1900s and slowly expanded to three stories. At its peak, it employed over 600 people. If you have ever had a pair of "Buster Brown" shoes, they could have been made there. I've also heard that they made gloves as well. Over a period of three years, I photographed there several times and never found a pair of shoes or even one glove! As this book is going to press, the City of Murphysboro has contracted someone to tear it down, and on my last visit, it was almost gone.

A side view showing how massive the building is.

Walls crumbling away. You can see the remains of an old freight elevator.

Inside the power plant area showing two large boilers.

Looking through a window. If you look closely, you can see the reflection of an exterior wall.

Part of the roof that has caved in.

One of my favorite photographs showing old wood in the power plant room.

Up-close view of one of the boilers.

Another view of the boilers showing how large they are. I would imagine that the building was built around them.

Looking up through the debris.

Another shot of the boilers. As you can tell, I am quite fascinated with these!

Using a little digital art on the interior with the trees growing inside the building.

The large smokestack behind the power plant.

I have no clue what this large blob is. Notice the cool old sliding doors behind the blob.

Drone shot showing the roof caved in and exposing only the exterior walls.

Drone view getting up close to the old freight shaft.

Drone view showing the huge smokestack and the decay of what is left of the building.

Ground view showing some old wood and holes in the ceiling.

This is another one of my personal favorites. I have positioned the drone directly above one building, showing the sheer devastation. Only the exterior walls remain.

A great view showing how large this building is.

Above: Another angle of the entire complex. Note the building on the right is in better shape, so possibly it will not be demolished.

Left: View from the very top of the huge smokestack. Notice how the metal band is starting to come apart.

This view reminds one of a building that was bombed during World War II. I still find there is beauty in decay.

Endgame. All that is left is a pile of bricks and the smokestack.

Getting near the end of the demolition, you can see how large this smokestack is.

2

FIRE AT 409 WEST MAIN STREET, CARBONDALE, ILLINOIS

Early in the morning of Tuesday, November 13, 2018, I received a phone call from my daughter, Katie, who asked what was going on at 409 West Main. She said that there were fire trucks all over the place, and there must be a fire. I immediately got ready to head into town and then my phone started ringing and ringing. The building was indeed burning. By the time I got there, flames and smoke were leaping into the sky and firemen were running all over the place.

As I stood there watching this, it brought back all kinds of memories. I purchased this apartment building back in 1980. I had my real estate appraisal office in it for several years and even lived in one of the apartments for a few months. It was a very special place to me.

Built in 1881 by Samuel Dunaway, this was considered a fabulous home with its Italianate architecture, huge windows, and tall ceilings. In the rear were horse stables and a fine brick courtyard. This old picture shows the house in its original form.

A photograph of how the original building appeared. The date and photographer is unknown. It is very old.

Over the years, it passed through several owners and sometime in the 1950s, the house was expanded and turned into apartments. The next two pictures show the living room and the library, which are very ornate. It was a very beautiful place.

Rumor has it that one of the previous owners hid silver dollars in one of the fireplaces, though I can say that I have looked and never found anything. I did manage to save the marble fireplace and the red etched glass over the front door.

A view of what was once the living room and library. Note the large doors and chandelier. It is my guess this photo was taken in the 1950s. Photographer unknown.

Interior view of what was once the library. Check out the neat fireplace and all the bookshelves. I am not sure who the man in the large picture is, but it could be Burnett Shryock.

Exterior of the front of the building showing how it looked prior to the fire. This photo is probably twenty-five to thirty years old. Photographer unknown.

This is the first thing I saw as I pulled into the back parking lot.

My personal favorite, showing all the action and hard work of the firemen trying to save the building. Who says an iPhone cannot take great pictures!

MILLER
CARBONDALE

MAYER

Above: The firemen talk it over while the ladder truck blasts the roof with literally thousands of gallons of water. Notice the water coming out of the front door. This photo was digitally enhanced to show just how dramatic this was.

Opposite above: Firemen climbing on a ladder truck as the water flies.

Opposite below: With the fire blazing, brave firemen are climbing on the roof in a desperate attempt to control the blaze.

Before the fire was almost out, the ladder truck kept pounding the roof with blasts of water. When the fire was out, the lower floor apartments had over 3 feet of water in them!

The ladder truck keeps pouring it on.

Same angle as the picture before, but in this one, you can actually see the flames inside the smoke. At this point there is not much anyone can do. The interior of the building is gone.

Black-and-white photo showing the damage and the machinery that will be torn down.

Total devastation. Check out the books on the bookshelf.

She still stands even though the inside and rear are heavily damaged. To me, this photograph shows the strength and beauty of this grand old building.

One section of the building after the fire was totally out.

View showing the brick flue and the large vent stack that is still on top of the building.

What remains of the library. You can still see the bookcases. This photo was taken after a snow.

Another of my favorites taken on the staircase looking up toward the blue sky. If you look closely, you can see some snow on the rail of the staircase.

The rear portion in process of being torn down.

The fireplace in what was once the master bedroom on the second floor. It was quite an experience to photograph.

An up-close shot showing the bookshelves that survived this horrific fire.

Sheer destruction during demolition.

Another shot during demolition.

An inside shot after the fire, which shows the original staircase still intact.

Inside the front door after the fire, showing the beautiful red etched glass. I did manage to remove and save it.

Machinery working to tear down the building.

A stylish shot using a wide-angle lens showing a section still standing.

It is crunch time. Another favorite showing the strength of the building that still remains, proudly showing 409.

3

JEFFERSON MEMORIAL HOSPITAL, MT. VERNON, ILLINOIS

This building was originally the offices for the Mt. Vernon Car Company. They built railroad cars, and at one time had over 1,000 employees. During World War II, they built shell casings. This business was started in 1889 and lasted until after the war. The building was then converted to a hospital in 1947 and closed in 1979.

Exterior view of the old hospital. Trust me, the building is much worse inside.

The last thing you expect to see in an old abandoned hospital. This old train set was quite a surprise, to say the least.

An old stairway leading up to the second floor. It was very dangerous, as you can see how it is leaning.

Using rich colors, I captured this shot with good lighting. It is some type of hospital equipment.

Above: The old coal fire boiler that provided heat to the building. There is still coal in the hopper.

Right: I dig that green floor, a sure sign of the roofing leaking.

An old stairway that I managed to go down. I basically had to walk the plank.

Another surprise: an old church pew. If they ever had a service there, I am sure someone got wet.

A rusted electrical box with the framing of a neat old doorway.

A different view of the furnace room.

Old hospitals contain the strangest things!

Some type of hospital equipment. I would be interested to know what this thing is.

Neat shot of an arched doorway leading to the stairs. The colors on this one really pop.

The last bed available. This hospital only had one bed with no mattress. I don't think I would want to get treated here!

Here it is again, only from a different angle. Upon closer inspection, I think this was once some type of concession trailer. Pretty cool!

The front of the building looking up.

4

LOCK AND DAM #53, OLMSTED, ILLINOIS

I came upon this place and found it very interesting. Built in 1929, the lock and dam were sort of self-contained, in that at one time, most of the workers lived on site in furnished houses. As you can see from the pictures, the large brick house was probably for the head guy, while the workers lived in the smaller modest white bungalows. The property was fenced off, so I had to use the drone to look. One time I was there, the river had flooded the control house and it was half underwater. This was a "wicket" dam and has been in use since 1929. They have now built a new lock and dam just downstream on the Ohio River.

This is where some of the workers stayed while working at lock and dam number 53.

A drone shot showing the large brick house where I would assume the boss man lived, and the rest of the workers' houses.

Right: Black-and-white drone shot that looks like it was taken fifty years ago. I definitely like the water tower.

Below: The machine room and office during a recent flood. If you look closely, you can see the water gauge on the front of the building showing the water level at almost 59 feet.

The back of the same building after the floodwaters had receded. Notice all the debris and stuff that the flood left by the building.

Up close on the boss's house. It sure is much nicer than the workers' houses.

The drone almost sitting right on top of the water tower during the flood. Check out the weathervane on top of the tower.

This is what a wicket dam actually looks like. This photo was taken upstream at lock and dam number 52.

The front of the complex showing that this facility was built in 1929.

5

THE WONDERS OF SOUTHERN ILLINOIS

Frankenstein's castle. Big disappointment, Frankenstein wasn't home! There were a bunch of weird birds.

The town of Thebes during a flood, backlit with a beautiful sunset. If you need gasoline, I suggest you go elsewhere.

Just a bunch of guys chillin' out in Cobden.

What is left of downtown Tamms. This was quite a hopping place back in the day.

Who has ever heard of Robb's? Well, they had a car dealership back in 1929. I bet the salesmen cheated you!

Weigh station at an abandoned rock quarry. Yes, the scale is still there. There was a railroad spur line that ran in front of the building.

Another gem from Robbs: this time, the inside of a gymnasium at an abandoned school.

This is all that is left from an old Illinois Central icehouse in Bluford. They used the ice as a way of refrigeration for the boxcars.

Above: A drone shot of the tower and all that remains from the old Illinois Central yard at Bluford.

Left: Don't end up here. This is the jail where Charlie Burger spent has last days. You don't get much bathroom privacy in this Benton jail!

Just a tranquil scene in the Catch River area.

Now I have seen it all: a movie theater turned into a plumbing shop. I wonder if they show you a movie if you give them a big plumbing order.

A super cool old grain building. I think it says Ty Williams Grain Company, but I'm not really sure.

Right: A photograph of massive proportions in Reevesville. This Illinois Central coaling tower still stands after many years. I'm told they are too expensive to tear down.

Below: Which one of these books would you pick?

A strange find: a movie projector in a field. It could be an old drive-in movie projector. I'm not sure about this one.

A drone shot taken at the old Illinois Central railroad bridge in Cairo. There are two modes of transportation here: the barges and the railroad. Without the drone, I could have never taken this unique shot.

Beautiful shot of the Illinois Central railroad bridge north of Carbondale. What great lines and what a massive bridge. It was built in 1902 and is still in use!

This is a retro gas station in Vienna. Standard Oil, no less.

You would never guess what this is. It is the inside of an old grain elevator. I love the coloring, especially the water at the bottom.

If you are looking for a room in Vienna, please check out the Dixon Motel. They have dial phone and cable TV. I bet the rates are reasonable!

The iconic bank in Old Shawneetown (as seen on the cover). What a beauty. Taken by my drone.

One of my better drone shots of what looks like the moon, or maybe even Mars. I am really surprised my little drone could fly that far. It is really an old coal mining site in Franklin County.

In what looks like some type of transformer, this black-and-white photo actually shows a piece of old coal mining equipment.

Old Illinois Central railroad car now used as storage in the CN railroad yard in Carbondale. I think it was a baggage car.

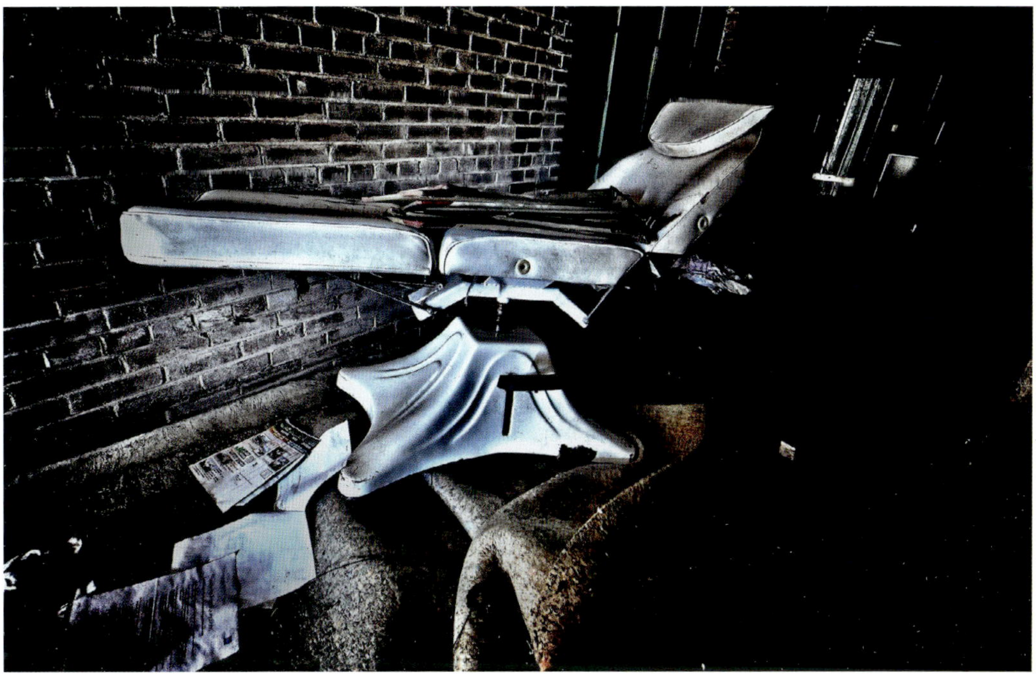

Yikes! Imagine coming across this old chair in a pitch-dark building. I didn't want any quack working on me. I am out of here!

Above: A lot of reflections and contrast at this barge facility in Cairo. I had the drone almost sitting right on top of the water. Barges are repaired here.

Left: This is one gorgeous church, the Saint Loasaph of Belgorod Orthodox Church near Muddy. It was built around 1913. Too bad I could not get inside.

The photo says it all.

Another of my favorite shots showing a unique angle of what is left of an old building in Hamilton County. I think this used to be an oil facility.

This is one unique photo. It looks like the lost tomb of the ancient aliens. I see what looks like two lit candles and a sword coming down from the top. Draw your own conclusions.

An interesting perspective of an old factory. The wood floors are warped from a leaking ceiling, and I was almost attacked by a bunch of pigeons!

As the sign says, when you use this restroom, "Please throw toilet paper in the toilet and flush after every use."

Black-and-white photograph of an old country store. The doors are open, but nobody was home.

Who would dare go down this strange stairway? I did. Indiana Mike made me do it.

Now this one was a challenge. I first had to climb a very steep hill to get to the building, then had to navigate my way inside and climb many flights of stairs to get to the top. It was a type of a quarry, as the top had a ramp into the cliff.

A pile of chains and rollers found in an abandoned factory.

A grain mill along the Ohio River.

Yikes! Every now and then you come across this when you are least expecting it. I don't know what is was and really don't want to know. It was about four feet long and had big teeth! My sidekicks have guessed everything but a human.

An old school gymnasium where the bleachers have fallen through the floor.

Left: Who likes old trains? Here are a whole bunch of engines waiting to be either rebuilt or scrapped.

Below: The old coaling towers in Carbondale, taken from where the old Roundhouse used to be.

Who can do a book about Southern Illinois without the Crenshaw house, otherwise known as the "old slave house"?

Inside of an old mechanical room at the Brookport Lock and Dam. You can tell this has not been used for a long time.

Above: Some exhaust equipment on top of the old Spartan Printing building in Sparta. I used to work there after high school.

Left: Part of an Otis elevator at the top of an old office building.

Right: A very up-close shot of some broken glass, complete with a few insects. I usually don't do macro photography, but I really like this one.

Below: America's Stonehenge? Well, it did make for a cool shot.

Can you guess what this weird bug thing is? It is part of an alarm system on an old bank in Old Shawneetown.

What is left of the housing projects in Cairo.

Above: The graffiti adds a little color to this old water treatment plant west of Jonesboro.

Right: If you need a place to store your money, I have the perfect place. Just be sure to give me the combination in case you might forget.

Above: Inside the mechanical room at a fluorite mine in Elizabethtown. This is where my first drone crashed and burned.

Left: This is spooky with the trees growing up the sides of the building. No thanks. I did not go in.

I found this to be quite humorous. Believe it or not, this was found in an old bank.

A bit of Americana.

Left: This ominous building was once part of a candy factory. I do not know the name of the candy. Rumor has it that this place is haunted.

Below: Great find in an abandoned church. I believe the photo tells all.

Oh my! Look what I found. A hangman's noose. I am not sure what happened here and think I do not want to know.

Abandoned art. I like the coffee pot!

Another old factory interior view filled with warped wooded floors and full of all types of things.

On my last expedition before this book was due to go to press, I found this in an old abandoned school. It looks like some type of shrine to me.

FINAL NOTE

My travels have taken me down many country roads, across fields, and through the skies in search of abandoned and unusual things. It has been rewarding and frustrating. I hope that I have shown you something you may have never seen or known about. The good news: this is not the end, as I will be starting on my second book shortly. To keep up with what I am doing, be sure to follow me on Facebook (Michael Wright Photographer).